EXPLORING ARTIFICIAL INTELLIGENCE

AI SAFETY

Elsie Olson

Lerner Publications ◆ Minneapolis

Lerner Publications Company
An imprint of Lerner Publishing Group, Inc.
241 First Avenue North
Minneapolis, MN 55401 USA

For reading levels and more information, look up this title at www.lernerbooks.com.

Main body text set in Aptifer Sans LT Pro.
Typeface provided by Linotype AG.

Designer: Viet Chu **Photo Editor:** Lucien Brinkley
Lerner team: Martha Kranes

Library of Congress Cataloging-in-Publication Data

Names: Olson, Elsie, 1986– author.
Title: AI safety / Elsie Olson.
Description: Minneapolis : Lerner Publications, [2025] | Series: Exploring artificial intelligence | Includes bibliographical references and index. | Audience: Ages 8–12 | Audience: Grades 4–6 | Summary: "Artificial intelligence is an incredible tool capable of impressive feats, but it also brings many safety concerns. Readers will examine some of them and learn to think critically about AI in this engaging exploration"— Provided by publisher.
Identifiers: LCCN 2024017951 (print) | LCCN 2024017952 (ebook) | ISBN 9798765647882 (lib. bdg.) | ISBN 9798765661659 (pbk.) | ISBN 9798765654439 (epub)
Subjects: LCSH: Artificial intelligence—Juvenile literature.
Classification: LCC Q335.4 .O475 2025 (print) | LCC Q335.4 (ebook) | DDC 006.3—dc23/eng/20240628

LC record available at https://lccn.loc.gov/2024017951
LC ebook record available at https://lccn.loc.gov/2024017952

Manufactured in the United States of America
1-1011013-53349-8/5/2024

TABLE OF CONTENTS

INTRODUCTION

SHAPING AI ETHICS

Sneha Revanur speaks in New York City.

Sneha Revanur was a first-year college student in 2023. She saw her classmates relying more and more on artificial intelligence (AI). Tech company OpenAI had released ChatGPT in 2022. Revanur saw her peers using the chatbot for almost everything. She worried AI technology was developing too fast. Something could go wrong. Her generation would be heavily impacted.

Revanur was no stranger to activism or to AI. While in high school, she founded Encode Justice. The organization advocated for safe and human-centered AI.

That summer youth activists attended congressional hearings about AI. A senator asked anyone younger than thirty-five to raise their hands. Gasps echoed through the room as most hands shot up.

Senate judiciary subcommittee hearing on AI

Vice President Kamala Harris

In July 2023, US vice president Kamala Harris invited Revanur to a roundtable discussion about AI risks. Revanur was the youngest attendee. She got to help shape the future of AI ethics for the next generation.

CHAPTER 1

FROM SCIENCE FICTION TO SCIENCE FACT

AI is the ability for a computer to mimic human intelligence. People have been thinking about AI since the early 1900s. Science fiction looked at how AI might impact humans. Isaac Asimov published *I, Robot*, a collection of short stories, in 1950. It influenced the way many people looked at AI. It even affected future laws about AIs.

The Three Laws of Robotics

In *I, Robot*, Asimov created the three laws of robotics. AIs must follow these rules to protect humans. The stories in *I, Robot* are fiction. But these laws have influenced real-life AI:

1. A robot may not injure a human or allow one to be harmed.

2. A robot must obey any order given by a human unless it conflicts with the first law.

3. A robot must protect itself unless it conflicts with the first or second law.

Technology Advances

While Asimov was writing, researchers were developing real-life AI. Computer scientists tested early AI computer programs through the 1960s.

Computers were not as powerful as they are now. And they were very expensive. The first AIs could do only simple tasks. They could solve math problems. Computer scientists had lots of ideas about what AI could do. But they lacked the technology to develop them.

In the 1960s, computers could take up most of a room!

A woman works on a computer in the early 1980s.

Customers interact with a new Apple computer for sale in 1998.

From the 1970s to the 1990s, computer scientists continued to push AI research forward. But the kind of AI Asimov had imagined still seemed far away. Yet technology improved throughout the early years of the 2000s.

Computers were more powerful than ever. The kinds of

thinking machines Asimov had described seemed to be in reach. Some people began to worry. They thought the technology could become too powerful.

Discussing the Future

In 2015 AI experts from around the world gathered in Puerto Rico for a private conference. They discussed the future of AI. Computer scientists had made great leaps in artificial neural networks. This machine learning is modeled on the human brain. It uses an algorithm that passes information through a network. This allows a computer to adapt and learn from its mistakes.

Attendees gather in Puerto Rico in 2015 to discuss AI's future.

Stephen Hawking

Neural networks had caused AI progress to race forward. Some felt it was moving too fast. Attendees of the conference signed an open letter. It called for more research into the possible impacts of AI. Signers included physicist Stephen Hawking, Tesla CEO Elon Musk, and philosopher Nick Bostrom.

IN THE SPOTLIGHT

NICK BOSTROM

Swedish philosopher Nick Bostrom studies the future of humanity. He published *Superintelligence* in 2014. This book warns about the dangers of AI becoming smarter than humans. Bostrom has published many papers on this topic. He published *Deep Utopia* in 2024. It looks at AI from an optimistic angle. The book considers a future where a supersmart AI benefits humans.

CHAPTER 2

AI SAFETY

In fall 2023, journalists gathered at the White House. They heard US president Joe Biden introduce an executive order he had signed. Its goal was to protect US citizens from the dangers of AI. Biden believed AI had potential but also posed great risks.

The executive order issued new rules to AI companies. It required them to tell the US government about the risks of AI. It also sought to limit the use of deepfakes. These are AI-created likenesses of real people. Deepfakes can include images, audio clips, and videos. Biden said they could be used to spread misinformation.

President Joe Biden signs the executive order on AI.

In January 2024, a deepfake had affected Biden personally. A robocall featuring Biden's voice called voters in New Hampshire. It encouraged them not to vote. The call was a deepfake. But many voters believed it was real. It raised concerns. AI could possibly influence politics.

Unlawful Activity

AI deepfakes became popular with criminals. Deepfakes could help criminals get past security programs. Some criminals used deepfakes of celebrities. They advertised products and services. They didn't have the celebrity's consent.

The distorted areas on the face of 44th US president Barack Obama show the process of creating a deepfake.

Cybercriminals also used AI to guess passwords. It could craft phishing emails and phone calls. Phishing attacks occurred during the 2023 holiday season. Cybercriminals used ChatGPT to write emails. They appeared to be from popular stores. The emails told people to enter their personal information to buy products at sale prices. But the emails were scams.

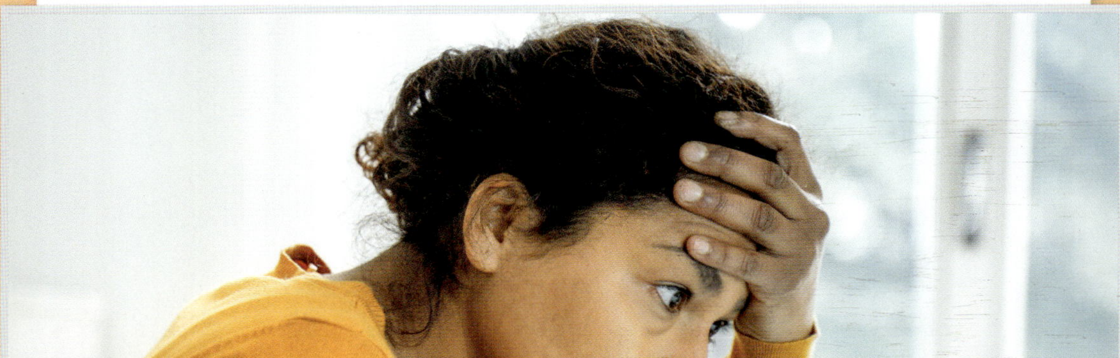

Cybercriminals may use AI in scams online and over the phone.

Ethics and Privacy

Many experts share concerns about AI's threat to privacy. Laws exist to protect a person's right to privacy. But these laws often don't apply to new technologies. AI algorithms are trained on data from the internet. AI companies don't always share details about this data. This includes where it comes from and how it's used and stored.

Artist Kelly McKernan is one of the artists suing AI companies for using their art as material to produce AI art.

AI can analyze large amounts of data fast. An AI could be trained to target someone. It could learn a lot about them using their digital footprint. This is information everyone leaves behind when they use the internet. It includes emails sent, photos posted, and much more. It could be used to spy on someone. Cybercriminals could even use this data to steal an identity.

Other AI critics have ethical concerns. AI companies don't get permission when using online data for their algorithms. Many artists and writers have argued that AI companies steal their work.

IN THE SPOTLIGHT

JOY BUOLAMWINI

In 2016 computer scientist and activist Joy Buolamwini founded the Algorithm Justice League. It focuses on the possible harms of AI. One of Buolamwini's greatest concerns is bias. She believes that racism, sexism, and other biases in AI will harm many communities. In 2023 she explored these issues in a book, *Unmasking AI: My Mission to Protect What Is Human in a World of Machines.*

Many computer scientists, politicians, and others are working to make sure people have access to safe and equitable technology.

Critics argued that AIs often show bias in their responses. This is because the data AI is trained on contains biases. This leads the AI to overlook many people's experiences. It can even promote stereotypes.

Arati Prabhakar (*left*), Director of the White House Office of Science and Technology Policy, takes the oath of office.

CHAPTER 3

FIGHTING BACK

In October 2022, the Blueprint for an AI Bill of Rights was released by the White House Office of Science and Technology Policy. It was made to protect AI users and to prevent discrimination and bias. But it only applied to the US federal government. Tech companies were not required to follow it. Supporters still believed it was a good first step. They felt it would help to make AI safe, beneficial, and equitable.

The AI Bill of Rights

The Blueprint for an AI Bill of Rights has five main points:

1. Users should be protected from unsafe or ineffective systems.

2. Users should not face discrimination when using algorithms, and systems should be equitable.

3. Users should be protected from harmful data practices and should have input in how data about them is used.

4. Users should understand when AI is being used and how it impacts them.

5. Users should not be required to use AI and should be able to access a human when problems occur.

Keeping People Safe

Many people are working to make AI safe. AI experts want future AI to benefit society. Some AI companies have made teams. The teams try to make sure their AI stays beneficial. They try to steer AI technology away from bias and discrimination.

A cabinet meeting takes place in the White House on October 2, 2023. Government officials are among those working to make AI safe.

Organizations such as Encode Justice and the Algorithmic Justice League also work to protect people from AI's harms. The organization Humane Intelligence holds contests for hackers. It challenges them to find ways to make AI algorithms act harmfully. AI companies can then fix these problems.

Many groups are working hard. They want to keep AI safe. But there are other important ways to keep AI safe.

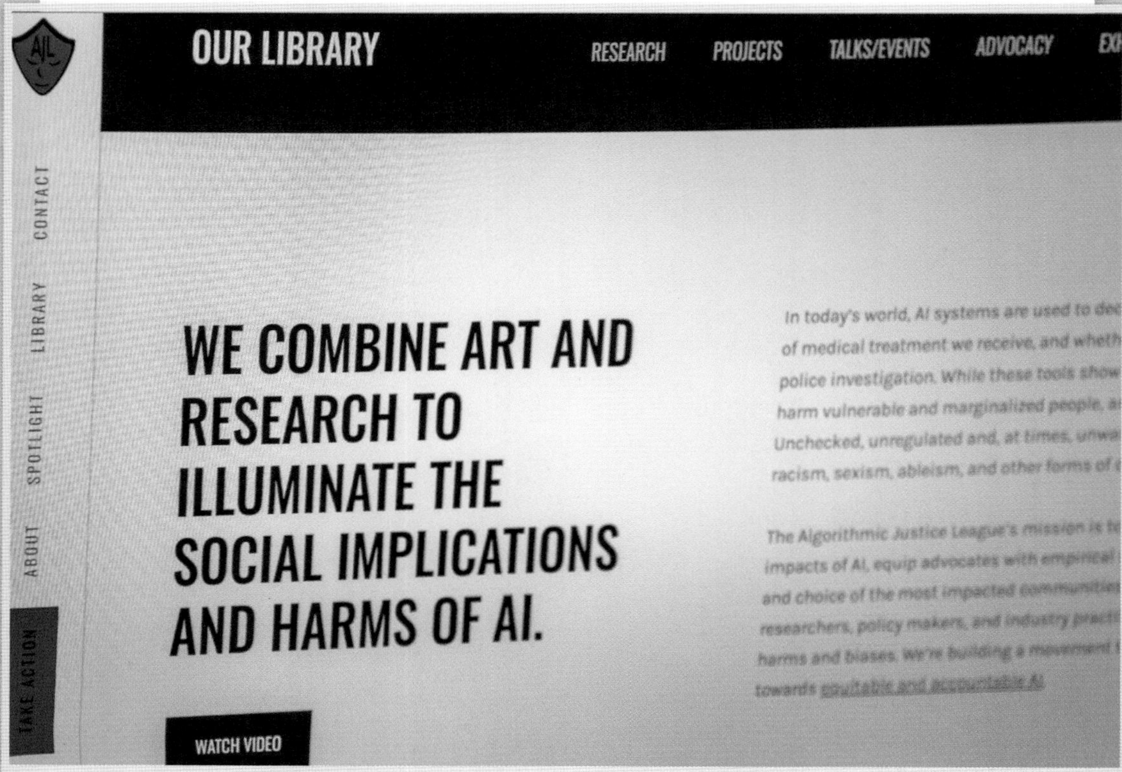

The Algorithmic Justice League website

Rumman Chowdhury (*standing, center*), leader of Humane Intelligence, talks with college students in 2023.

Its users can protect themselves by following a few rules: Start by considering how to protect your privacy. Check the privacy settings for the websites you visit. Be mindful of the personal information you share online. This includes what you share on social media. Consider how it may be used. If you see biased or inappropriate content while using an AI, report it to the developers.

Looking Ahead

An important guideline is to check the information you get from AI. Don't use AI as your only source of information. AI-generated content can be biased, discriminatory, or wrong. Check information you get from an AI against a reputable source. AI bases its content on the works of millions of people. It may not all be correct.

AI has exciting possibilities when it's developed and used responsibly.

AI is an exciting technology. It has the potential to make our world a better place. But we must make sure it is developed safely and ethically. Computer scientists, tech companies, governments, and activists are working together to do that. They want future AI to benefit everyone.

Glossary

advocate: to publicly recommend or support something

algorithm: a set of rules or instructions for solving a problem

bias: the assumption that something is a certain way based on past experience or preexisting beliefs rather than on factual information

chatbot: a computer program designed to simulate human conversation when interacting with a human

equitable: fair and equal treatment for everyone

ethical: behaving in a way that is good for society and shows honesty and good judgment

phishing: sending fraudulent emails designed to steal a recipient's personal information

program: instructions given to a computer using computer code, or the act of giving a computer those instructions

scam: a fraudulent or deceptive act or operation

stereotype: an idea that many people have about a thing or a group that may often be untrue or partly true

Learn More

Britannica Kids: Artificial Intelligence (AI)
https://kids.britannica.com/students/article/artificial-intelligence-AI/272968

Hudak, Heather C. *Cybercrime*. Minneapolis: Core Library, 2020.

Kiddle: Artificial Intelligence Facts for Kids
https://kids.kiddle.co/Artificial_intelligence

National Geographic Kids: Could a Robot Become President?
https://kids.nationalgeographic.com/books/article/could-a-robot-become-president

Olson, Elsie. *AI Basics*. Minneapolis: Lerner Publications, 2025.

Owings, Lisa. *Robot Uprising*. Minneapolis: Bellwether Media, 2020.

Sneha Revanur
https://time.com/collection/time100-ai/6310595/sneha-revanur/

Spilsbury, Louise. *Robots Enforcing the Law*. Shrewsbury, UK: Cheriton Children's Books, 2024.

Index

Photo Acknowledgments

Image credits: Roy Rochlin/Getty Images, p. 4; Graeme Sloan/Sipa USA via AP Images, p. 5; US Embassy/State Department Photo/Alamy Live News, p. 6; Mondadori via Getty Images, p. 7; Retro AdArchives/Alamy, p. 8; Keystone/Getty Images, p. 9; Dwight Ellefsen/FPG/Archive Photos/Getty Images, p. 10 (top); Sean Gallup/Getty Images, p. 10 (bottom); Courtesy of The Future of Life Institute (FLI), p. 11; Eleanor Bentall/Corbis via Getty Images, p. 12; Tom Pilston for The Washington Post via Getty Images, p. 13; AP Photo/Evan Vucci, pp. 14, 15; 5m3photos/Getty Images, p. 16; AP Photo p. 17; Visions/Getty Images, p. 18; Kosamtu/Getty Images, p. 19; AP Photo/George Walker IV, p. 20; Marla Aufmuth/Getty Images, p. 21; VioletaStoimenova/Getty Images, p. 22; Yuri Gripas/Abaca/Bloomberg via Getty Images, p. 23; Official White House Photo by Adam Schultz, p. 25; Independent Picture Service, p. 26; Marvin Joseph/The Washington Post via Getty Images, p. 27; SeventyFour/Getty Images, p. 28; Yevhen Shkolenko/Alamy, p. 29. Design elements: filo/Getty Images; JakeOlimb/Getty Images.

Cover: Peter Dazeley/Getty Images.